Published in 2013 by The Rosen Publishing Group, Inc.
29 East 21st Street, New York, NY 10010

Photo Credits: **KEY** tl=top left; tc=top center; tr=top right; cl=center left; c=center; cr=center right; bl=bottom left; bc=bottom center; br=bottom right

Photo Credits: **KEY** tl=top left; tc=top center; tr=top right; cl=center left; c=center; cr=center right; bl=bottom left; bc=bottom center; br=bottom right; bg=background
CBT = Corbis; DT = Dreamstime; GI = Getty Images; iS = istockphoto.com; SH = Shutterstock; TF = Topfoto

front cover bg SH; bl TF; **back cover** cl GI; bc SH; **2-3**bg CBT; **4-5**bg CBT; **6**bl, tc iS; **7**tl iS; bl, br, tr SH; **8**bl iS; tr SH; **8-9**cr GI; **9**br DT; **10**bl iS; **10-11**bg SH; **11**bl iS; br SH; **12-13**bg CBT; **13**br iS; **14-15**bg CBT; tc SH; **15**cr CBT; br, tr iS; **16-17**bg iS; **17**tr DT; **18**bl TF; **19**tr CBT; br iS; **20**bl, cr TF; **20-21**c CBT; bg iS; **21**cr SH; tc TF; **22-23**bc CBT; **23**cr TF; **24-25**tr SH; **25**bl CBT; **26**bc, br, br iS; cl TF; **27**bc, bc, bc, bl, bl, br, br iS; cr SH; **28**bl CBT; tc, tc, tc, tr, tr, tr, tr iS; cr SH; **28-29**bg iS; **29**tr iS; **30**bc, br, cr SH; **30-31**bg SH; **32**bg iS **18-19**; **22-23**; **24**c Lionel Portier

All illustrations copyright Weldon Owen Pty Ltd.

Weldon Owen Pty Ltd
Managing Director: Kay Scarlett
Creative Director: Sue Burk
Publisher: Helen Bateman
Senior Vice President, International Sales: Stuart Laurence
Vice President Sales North America: Ellen Towell
Administration Manager, International Sales: Kristine Ravn

Library of Congress Cataloging-in-Publication Data
McAllan, Kate.
 Water is precious / by Kate McAllan. — 1st ed.
  p. cm. — (Discovery education: the environment)
 Includes index.
 ISBN 978-1-4488-7893-2 (library binding) — ISBN 978-1-4488-7981-6 (pbk.) —
ISBN 978-1-4488-7987-8 (6-pack)
 1. Water—Environmental aspects—Juvenile literature. I. Title.
 GB662.3.M3919 2013
 553.7—dc23
                                2011050236

Manufactured in the United States of America

CPSIA Compliance Information: Batch #SW12PK: For Further Information contact Rosen Publishing, New York, New York at 1-800-237-9932

Discovery
EDUCATION™

THE ENVIRONMENT

WATER IS PRECIOUS

KATE MCALLAN

PowerKiDS
press™

New York

Contents

A Watery World

Around two-thirds of Earth's surface is covered by water. Most of this is salty and is held in the oceans. About 3 percent of Earth's water is fresh, but two-thirds of that is frozen or is deep underground. All living things need water. Most organisms are adapted to life in salt water, though some rely on freshwater. Organisms are made up of cells, which are usually more than 75 percent water. Plants soak up water through their roots, carrying nutrients dissolved in the water to their cells. An animal's blood is mainly water. Blood carries dissolved oxygen, nutrients, and waste products around the body.

Life in a drop of water
Microorganisms such as this daphnia, or water flea, often live in water. Some species of daphnia are only 0.008 inch (0.2 mm) long.

The Dead Sea
The level of salt in the Dead Sea, between Israel and Jordan, is 10 times greater than normal seawater. This means that things float easily in it, but few organisms can survive there.

A body of water
Humans are made up of between 60 and 70 percent water. Our bodies cannot function if we go without clean freshwater for more than a week.

Groundwater
Water seeps down from Earth's surface and collects between rocks and soil, forming underground rivers in caves.

Lakes
Large bodies of water surrounded by land are called lakes. Freshwater lakes provide drinking water for millions of people.

Rivers
Water flows to the lowest point on land. Where plenty of water flows, rivers form.

Glaciers
In cold regions, rivers of ice and snow form. Called glaciers, these hold the greatest amounts of freshwater on Earth.

The Water Cycle

Water moves continually around Earth. When the Sun heats the surface of oceans, lakes, or rivers, water evaporates. This means it changes from a liquid to a gas called water vapor. When the air can hold no more water vapor, it condenses, becoming liquid again. This often happens when the air is cold, as cold air holds less water vapor than warm air. As the water condenses, it forms droplets around dust and other tiny airborne particles. Groups of droplets form clouds. When the droplets become too large and heavy to be held up by gravity, they fall as dew, rain, snow, or hail.

Water carriers
Air currents move clouds around. The water and ice crystals they carry fall over land or over the sea.

Cloud formation
As water vapor rises, it condenses into water droplets that form clouds.

Thermal springs
Evaporation is usually invisible. However, at thermal springs, where heat from inside Earth makes water extremely hot, water vapor rises as steam.

Evaporation
As water is heated by the Sun, it changes into water vapor.

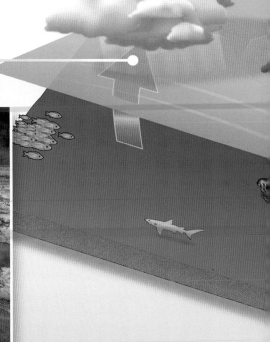

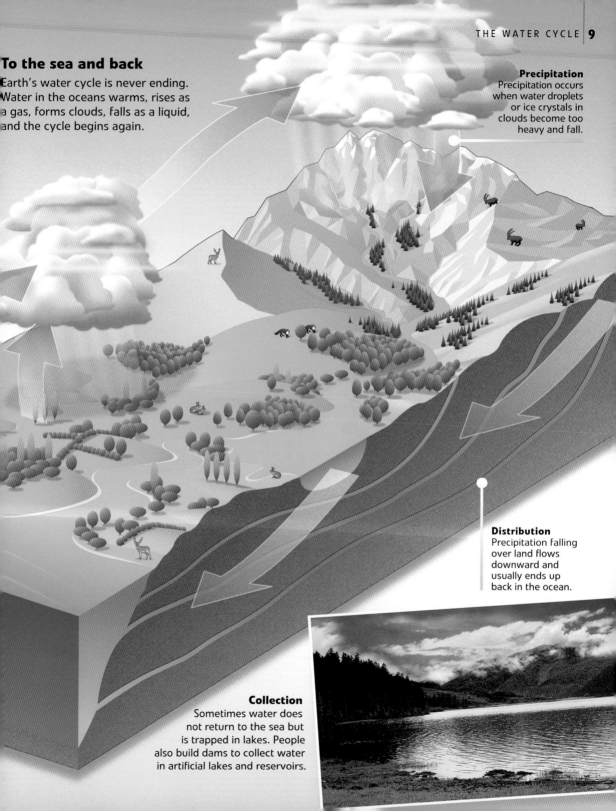

To the sea and back

Earth's water cycle is never ending. Water in the oceans warms, rises as a gas, forms clouds, falls as a liquid, and the cycle begins again.

Precipitation
Precipitation occurs when water droplets or ice crystals in clouds become too heavy and fall.

Distribution
Precipitation falling over land flows downward and usually ends up back in the ocean.

Collection
Sometimes water does not return to the sea but is trapped in lakes. People also build dams to collect water in artificial lakes and reservoirs.

Locked in Ice

W hen water freezes, it turns to ice. In mountainous areas and at Earth's North and South Poles, frozen water is a permanent feature of the landscape. In high regions and closer to the poles, winters bring snow and ice. Frozen environments present animals and plants with special challenges. When water turns to ice, it cannot carry nutrients and chemicals to and from their cells. Also, frozen water expands and ruptures cell walls, destroying them. If cells freeze, they stop working and the organism usually dies.

Trapped heating
The arctic fox has a thick winter coat, a layer of fat, and furry feet to stop it from losing its body heat.

Hidden heating

A polar bear's thick fur traps its body heat. Each hair is hollow, so sunlight reaches the bear's black skin, which absorbs the warmth.

Some Arctic insects have special blood that stops ice crystals from forming. They can survive temperatures well below freezing.

SHEDDING FOR WINTER

In the fall, the aspen tree slowly dries out, which makes its leaves turn yellow and drop off. This leaves less water in the tree's body to freeze and expand in winter. Also, the water that is left is sugary and freezes at a colder temperature.

Aspen trees in fall

Aspen trees in winter

Climate Change

The temperature of Earth's atmosphere has varied greatly over time. When it is colder, more water is locked up as ice and sea levels are lower. When it is warmer, the ice melts and seas rise, covering more land. Scientists have noticed that Earth's temperature seems to be increasing quickly. As ice melts, vast amounts of water will be unlocked, but this does not necessarily mean more freshwater will be available. Weather patterns are also showing signs of altering, and water availability is becoming more unpredictable.

ACROSS THE BERING STRAIT

Around 20,000 years ago, Earth's temperature was about 14° F (8°C) cooler than today. The sea level was about 400 feet (120 m) lower. Siberia and Alaska, now separated by 50 miles (80 km) of sea called the Bering Strait, were then joined by land. Herds of animals traveled from Asia to North America and hunters followed.

Trekking to America

Collapsing ice shelf

The ice shelves around Antarctica and the Arctic, as well as glaciers, are shrinking rapidly. Great chunks of ice often fall free. Scientists predict that, in the near future, so much ice will melt that sea levels will rise dramatically.

When sea levels rise
The Asian tsunami of 2004 struck India's east coast. At Mahabalipuram, massive amounts of sand were scoured away, uncovering ancient ruins under the sea. Sea level rises may have led to them being covered with water and sand.

Flood

Floods occur when large amounts of rain fall in short periods, when large amounts of snow and ice thaw quickly, or when storms push seawater ashore. Flooding can cause death and destruction and can be a regular event. For example, monsoons bring heavy rain to some areas each summer when winds from the ocean blow over the land, bringing moisture-laden air along with them. Random extreme weather events can also cause severe flooding.

Record floods

When floods struck southern China in 2008, 1.3 million people were evacuated and 252 people died. More than 5.4 million acres (2.2 million ha) of farmland were inundated, ruining crops.

Opening the floodgates

People in flood-prone areas can prepare for floods. Levee banks keep floodwater off built-up areas. Dams regulate water flow, capturing water that is used for drinking, irrigation, and making electricity. If heavy rains come, the floodgates are opened to release excess water. Care must be taken to tell people downstream that more water than usual is coming.

On stilts

Houses near Tonle Sap, Cambodia, stand on 20-foot-(6 m) high stilts so they will be clear of the lake's water during the wet season.

Annual floods

The Ganges River delta in Bangladesh has rich soil because of the silt carried by the annual floods. However, each year the riverbanks wash away, and many houses, fields, and lives are lost.

Land clearing

Forest soils are kept thick and spongy by rotting leaves and wood. When heavy rain falls, the soil soaks up much of the water. If forests are cleared, water rushes away, adding to floodwaters.

Drought zones
This map shows areas where drought was declared between 1980 and 2000.

KEY
Moderate
Severe
Extreme

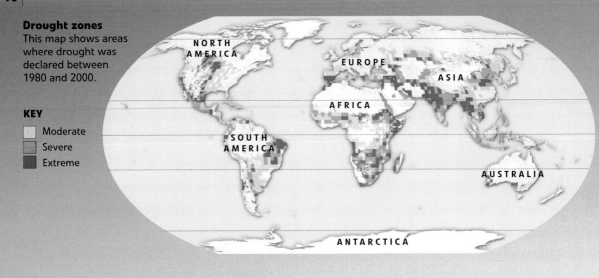

NORTH AMERICA

EUROPE

ASIA

AFRICA

SOUTH AMERICA

AUSTRALIA

ANTARCTICA

Drought

When an area has less precipitation than normal for a considerable time, we say it is in drought. If droughts go on for many years, they can be devastating. Famine is the worst effect of drought. People die of starvation and of illnesses they are too weak to fight. When rain returns, farmers often do not have the seeds they need to plant crops or the animals they need to breed new herds.

Transporting water
In drought-stricken South Dakota a pipeline is being built to bring water to farms from the Missouri River.

The Murray River

In eastern Australia, a drought lasting seven years has left the Murray River severely short of water. Farmers have not been able to grow crops. Scientists fear the river's ecosystem will not recover.

Dirty Water

Unfortunately, people have long dumped trash in water, letting rivers and oceans carry it away. Sometimes people deliberately pump sewage and factory pollutants into rivers and dump garbage out to sea. At other times, waste accidentally ends up in the water, such as when an oil spill occurs or when rain carries chemical and animal waste away as runoff. With the human population growing, pollution is increasing, and more freshwater is becoming too dirty to be used.

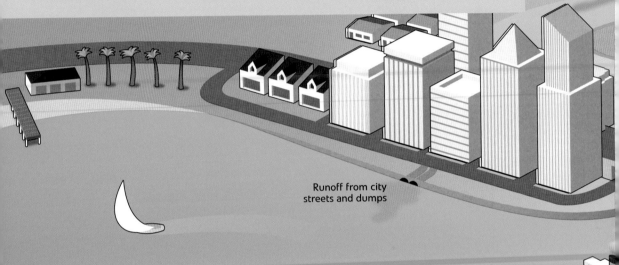

Runoff from city streets and dumps

Dumping at sea

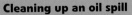

Oil spill from boat

Cleaning up an oil spill
In 2009, a power station in Siberia exploded, spilling oil into the Yenisei River. Steps were taken to clean it up, but farmed fish and wildlife were killed.

Wildlife hazard

Litter in water can harm wildlife. This gull has plastic caught around its head that may stop it from being able to eat.

Runoff from factories

Runoff from agricultural land

River discharging trash into sea

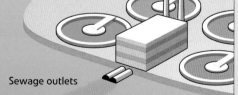

Floating trash

Sewage outlets

POLLUTED RIVER WATER

The historic Jordan River is one of the most polluted rivers in the world. It runs through Syria, Jordan, and Israel. All three nations take clean water from the river, reducing its flow by 90 percent. Raw sewage and other pollutants are pumped back into the river.

Columns in the murky Jordan River

All going somewhere

The sewage, chemical waste, and trash we dump in rivers and oceans do not disappear. They are carried somewhere else, often harming the ecosystem and other people.

Irrigation

Rainfall can be unpredictable. Farmers cannot always rely on it coming at the right time to grow their crops and support herds of grazing animals. For at least 5,000 years, farmers have been using irrigation to control water supplies. When rain falls, they capture the water behind dams. When dry times come, they use irrigation channels and pipes to take water from rivers and reservoirs to their fields, crops, and thirsty livestock.

China
Chinese farmers have long used a simple device, consisting of a bucket attached by a rope to a moving pole, to help lift water from one irrigation channel to another.

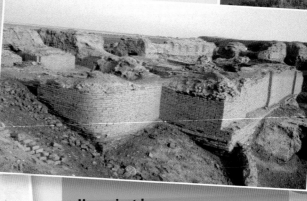

Ur, ancient Iraq
Ur, one of the first cities, is thought to have developed when the environment became drier and several farming communities came together to build irrigation systems. These tombs belonged to the city's rulers.

TO DAM OR NOT TO DAM

China's Three Gorges Dam, the world's largest, straddles the Yangtze River. The dam controls floodwaters and generates huge amounts of electricity. However, it has some downsides. The river's environment has changed, threatening rare wildlife. Pressure on surrounding land may also increase landslides. During its construction, many historic sites were lost and 1.2 million people had to be relocated.

Building the Three Gorges Dam in China

Angkor, Cambodia

The Khmer kingdom thrived due to an irrigation system that captured monsoon rains in reservoirs and enabled extensive rice farming. The kingdom may have collapsed, at least in part, because flood debris choked the irrigation channels.

Australia

In much of Australia, rainfall is irregular. Without stored water and irrigation, farming cannot take place. Irrigation pipelines are being introduced to reduce water loss caused by evaporation.

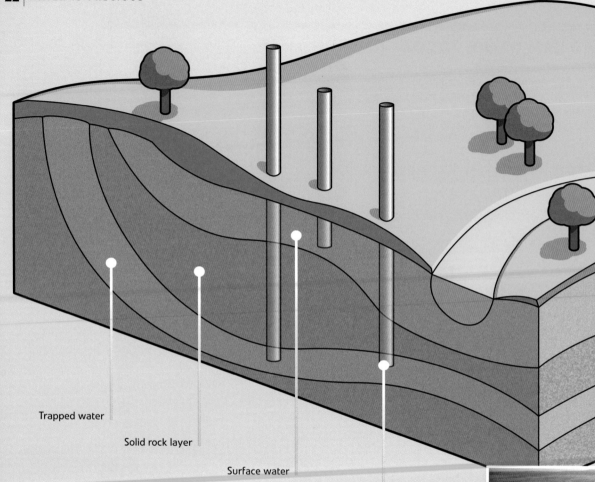

Trapped water

Solid rock layer

Surface water

Bore drilled to
reach water

Pump It Up

n some parts of the world there is limited surface water,
but deep under the ground lie hidden reservoirs. For example,
although Saudi Arabia has no rivers or lakes, aquifers lie beneath
its deserts. In the past, people dug wells to reach the water.
They lifted it to the surface using buckets. Now they dig deeper
with boring equipment and pump the water to the surface.
The water is used for drinking, agriculture, and industry.

Hidden reserves

Some rain that falls soaks deep into the ground. There it becomes trapped between layers of rock or in soil. Some of these underground reservoirs, or aquifers, have taken thousands of years to fill. People now pump the water to the surface to use.

Irrigating Israel

Even though much of Israel is desert, the country aims to grow its own food. To do this, it relies heavily on aquifers. Israel shares aquifers with other nations, and there is much conflict over water in the region.

Ogallala aquifer

This vast, shallow aquifer lies under nearly one-third of the United States' agricultural land. However, in some areas, the water has disappeared. It has been pumped up faster than it can be replaced.

Desalination

E arth's population is growing fast, but supplies of clean freshwater are shrinking. Many communities around the world are faced with water shortages. As well as finding ways to reduce their water usage, some populations now purify salt water, taking out the salt to leave fresh, desalinated water. This water is used for drinking and agriculture. Unfortunately, desalination consumes much energy, making the process expensive, and often contributes to pollution.

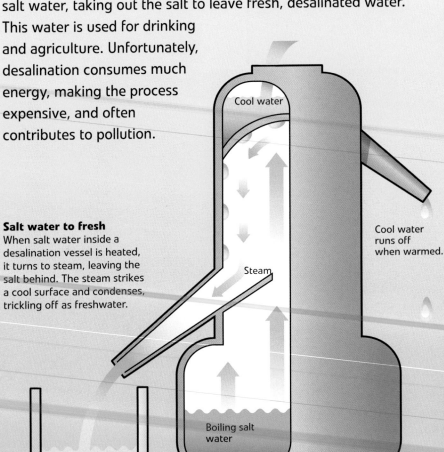

Salt water to fresh
When salt water inside a desalination vessel is heated, it turns to steam, leaving the salt behind. The steam strikes a cool surface and condenses, trickling off as freshwater.

Cool water

Cool water runs off when warmed.

Steam

Boiling salt water

Freshwater

Heat

Making water
Lanzarote, one of the Span
Canary Islands, is very dry.
When it became a tourist
destination during the 196
there was not enough wat
to supply all the hotels and
resorts. A desalination plar
was built, and now 99 per
of the freshwater people u
there comes from the plar

Water filters
At this desalination plant at Tampa Bay, the largest in North America, seawater goes through high-pressure filters to remove the salt.

Who Uses What?

All people use water, but people living in different places use different amounts. Some countries and communities use large amounts of water. Others use very little. The water we see, such as water used for washing, cleaning, and drinking, is not the only water we consume. Everything we eat or use takes water to produce. For example, to produce an egg, we need freshwater for the chicken to drink, water to grow the chicken feed, and water to produce the wood or metal to make the chicken shed.

Getting water
In many communities, it takes hard work to get water. People, usually women and children, must carry water from wells or rivers to their homes.

Did You Know?

Some countries that do not have much water import goods that need large amounts of water to make. For instance, Saudi Arabia imports wheat rather than growing it.

How much water?

One sheet of paper	One cup of coffee	One gallon of milk (4 l)
2.6 gallons (10 l)	40 gallons (150 l)	904 gallons (3,400 l)

Water footprints

A water footprint is how much water is used directly or indirectly per person per year in a given country. Footprint sizes vary widely between countries.

Russia	**65,614 cubic feet** (1,858 m³)
Australia	**56,751 cubic feet** (1,607 m³)
Brazil	**48,770 cubic feet** (1,381 m³)
Saudi Arabia	**44,602 cubic feet** (1,263 m³)
UK	**43,967 cubic feet** (1,245 m³)
Japan	**40,718 cubic feet** (1,153 m³)
Bangladesh	**31,642 cubic feet** (896 m³)
Peru	**27,439 cubic feet** (777 m³)
Kenya	**25,215 cubic feet** (714 m³)
China	**24,791 cubic feet** (702 m³)

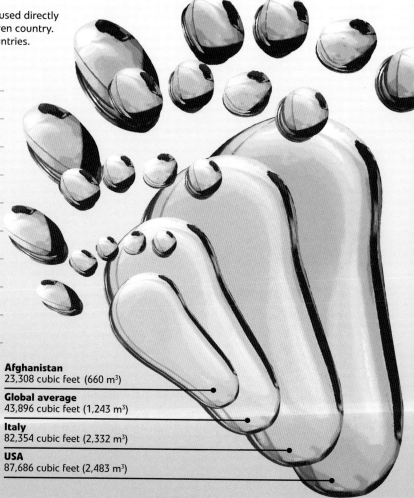

Afghanistan
23,308 cubic feet (660 m³)

Global average
43,896 cubic feet (1,243 m³)

Italy
82,354 cubic feet (2,332 m³)

USA
87,686 cubic feet (2,483 m³)

What we consume determines how much water we use. Compare how much it takes to make 2.2 pounds (1 kg) of these foods and other everyday items.

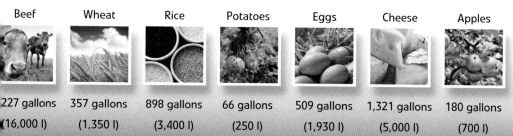

Beef	Wheat	Rice	Potatoes	Eggs	Cheese	Apples
3,227 gallons (16,000 l)	357 gallons (1,350 l)	898 gallons (3,400 l)	66 gallons (250 l)	509 gallons (1,930 l)	1,321 gallons (5,000 l)	180 gallons (700 l)

Saving Water

A ll living things need clean water. Earth's rapidly growing human population is putting a strain on the planet's water resources. We can all help to conserve the water we have and keep it clean for the future.

SUCCESSFUL SAVING

Melbourne, Australia, recently faced drought. Water supplies dwindled drastically and people were encouraged to use less water. The daily average water use per person soon decreased.

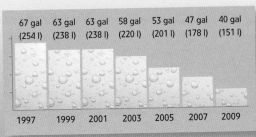

1997	1999	2001	2003	2005	2007	2009
67 gal (254 l)	63 gal (238 l)	63 gal (238 l)	58 gal (220 l)	53 gal (201 l)	47 gal (178 l)	40 gal (151 l)

Clean waterways
It is important to encourage everyone to keep waterways healthy and free of garbage.

Street cleaning
Recycled water can be used for jobs that do not need drinking-quality water.

HOW TO SAVE WATER EVERY DAY

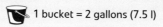 1 cup = 8 fluid ounces (240 ml)  1 bucket = 2 gallons (7.5 l) 1 faucet = 3 gallons (11 l) per minute

Bathroom

The average family turns on their home faucets 70 times a day. Most water waste happens in the bathroom.

Turn the faucet off while scrubbing hands, then quickly rinse.

Save 1.5 gallons (6 l).

Have a three-minute shower instead of a bath to save water.

Save 15 gallons (57 l).

Fill an empty soda bottle with water and put it in the toilet tank.

Save 1 quart (1 l) each flush.

Turn off the faucet while brushing your teeth.

Save 4 gallons (15 l).

Garden

It can be fun to help around the yard, but take it one step farther and start saving water here.

Rinse suds off the car with a bucket, not a hose.

Save 926 gallons (3,505 l).

Plant trees and flowers that do not need much water.

Save 80 percent of water usage.

Water the garden in the early morning so less water will evaporate.

Save 70 percent of water usage.

Instead of hosing down paths, sweep them with a broom.

Save 30 gallons (113 l).

Kitchen

Think before you act! Does that shirt really need to be washed? Can you turn off the faucet while doing a job?

Put only really dirty clothes in the laundry basket.

Save 11 gallons (42 l) per load.

Boil only the amount of water you need for a hot drink.

Save 1 quart (1 l).

Wash vegetables in a basin of water, not under a running faucet.

Save 3 gallons (11 l).

Run the dishwasher only when it is full.
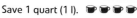
Save 6 gallons (23 l) per cycle.

Rain in a Jar

This easy experiment shows how rain forms.
Take care when using hot water.

What you need:

☑ One empty glass jar with lid

☑ Ice cubes

☑ Hot water

1 Fill the jar one third of the way with hot water from the faucet.

2 Put the jar's dry lid over the top, but place the lid upside down.

3 Place ice cubes in the upturned lid.

4 After a few minutes, what do you see on the underside of the lid?

When steam from the water rises and touches the cool lid, the water vapor turns back into water.

Glossary

aquifer (A-kwuh-fur) A layer of rock, gravel, or sand that holds water.

boring (BOR-ing) Drilling into or through.

cell (SEL) The most basic unit of all living things. It can be seen only with a microscope.

delta (DEL-tuh) A lowland area where a river meets the sea, spreading out into many channels.

ecosystem (EE-koh-sis-tem) All the interacting elements of an environment. In a river, this includes fish, plants, and microorganisms.

evacuated (ee-VA-kyoo-ayt-ed) Removed or made someone leave.

generate (JEH-neh-rayt) To produce.

inundated (IH-nun-dayt-ed) Flooded.

irrigation (ih-rih-GAY-shun) The supply of water to farmland through pipes or channels.

manufacture (man-yuh-FAK-cher) To make something, especially a large number of the same things, in an organized way.

monsoons (mon-SOON) Seasonal winds that bring heavy rain in Asia.

nutrients (NOO-tree-ents) Substances taken in by an organism in order to grow or to provide energy.

organisms (OR-guh-nih-zumz) Living things, from simple bacteria to complex animals.

plant (PLANT) A manufacturing complex, including the building and machinery.

pollutant (puh-LOO-tant) A harmful substance that is released into the environment.

reservoirs (REH-zuh-vwar) Storage areas for liquids, such as water.

resources (REE-sawrs-ez) Supplies of food, water, land, or valuable goods and materials.

runoff (RUN-of) Precipitation that does not soak into land but flows away.

rupture (RUP-cher) To break open or burst.

sewage (SOO-ij) The waste matter and water that is carried away from houses in pipes.

unpredictable (un-prih-DIK-tuh-bel) Not able to be known beforehand.

Index

A
Angkor, Cambodia 21
Antarctica 13
Arctic 11, 13
arctic fox 10
aspen tree 11

B
Bering Strait 13

C
cell 6, 10
clean water 6, 18, 28
clouds 8, 9

D
dam 9, 15, 20, 21
Dead Sea 6
desert 22, 23

E
evaporation 8, 21

F
freshwater 6, 7, 12, 18, 24–26

G
glaciers 7, 13

I
ice 7, 9, 10–13

L
lakes 7, 9, 15, 22
Lanzarote, Canary Islands 24

M
Mahabalipuram, India 13
Melbourne, Australia 28
monsoon 14, 21

O
oceans 6, 8 , 9, 14, 18, 19
Ogallala aquifer 23
oil 18

P
polar bear 11
poles 10
pollution 18–19, 24, 28
precipitation 9, 16

R
rain 8, 14, 15, 16, 18, 20, 21, 23
    30
recycled water 28
reservoirs 20, 21, 22, 23
river 7, 18, 19, 20, 22, 26
    Ganges River, Bangladesh 15
    Jordan River 19
    Murray River, Australia 17
    Yangtze River, China 21

S
salt water 6, 24–25
Saudi Arabia 22, 26, 27
sea levels 12, 13

T
Tampa Bay 25
Three Gorges Dam, China 21

U
Ur, Iraq 20

W
water vapor 8, 30

Websites

Due to the changing nature of Internet links, PowerKids Press has developed an online list of websites related to the subject of this book. This site is updated regularly. Please use this link to access the list: www.powerkidslinks.com/disc/water/